SRA
Reading Mastery®
Transformations

Reading
Workbook C

Siegfried Engelmann

Susie Andrist

Tina Wells

Mc
Graw
Hill

Acknowledgments

The authors are extremely grateful to Tina Wells for keeping the ship afloat on this project, and to Patricia McFadden, Margie Mayo, and Chris Gladfelter for their great attention to detail.

mheducation.com/prek-12

Send all inquiries to:
McGraw-Hill Education
8787 Orion Place
Columbus, OH 43240

ISBN: 978-0-07-905372-5
MHID: 0-07-905372-6

Printed in the United States of America.

2 3 4 5 6 7 8 9 10 LMN 26 25 24 23 22 21

A STORY ITEMS

1. In which month does this story take place? _____

2. Was Al happy about the test he had taken in school? _____

3. Did Al like school very much? _____

4. What did the sign in the store window say?

    _____

5. Who owned the store? _____

6. Does Al need money to pay for the trips the old man will take him on?

    _____

7. What does Al have to do to pay for his trips?

    _____

8. For Al's first trip, he wanted to go in a _____ because

    he liked to go _____ .

9. What will happen if Al passes a test the old man gives him?

    _____

10. What will happen if Al doesn't pass a test? _____

    _____

B SKILL ITEMS

Next to each word, write the word that means the opposite.

1. agree _____   3. like _____

2. appear _____   4. honest _____

| chilly | sick | inventor | problem | | electricity | need | invent |
| shopkeeper | pale | patent | manufacturers | invention | warm |

ACROSS

1. When you invent something, you start with a ▮▮▮▮ .

4. Businesses that make things are called ▮▮▮▮ .

5. The object that an inventor makes is called an ▮▮▮▮ .

6. An inventor gets a ▮▮▮▮ to protect an invention.

7. Another word for **sort of cold** is ▮▮▮▮ .

DOWN

2. Leonard's invention ran on ▮▮▮▮ .

3. The person who makes an object for the first time is called an ▮▮▮▮ .

6. Another way to say **light** blue is ▮▮▮▮ blue.

GO TO PART C IN YOUR TEXTBOOK

A INFORMATION ITEMS

1. How far does light travel in one second?

    • 86 miles

    • 186 thousand miles

    • 186 miles

2. What else travels as fast as light? _____

3. How long does it take light to travel from the sun to Earth?

    _____

B STORY ITEMS

1. What does Al have to do to pay for his trips?

    _____

2. Name the first vehicle Al and the old man rode in.

    _____

3. What was the fastest speed they went in that vehicle?

    • 500 miles per hour

    • 130 miles per hour

    • 200 miles per hour

4. Why did Al and the old man have to shout in the racing car?

    _____

5. Name the second vehicle Al and the old man rode in.

    _____

6. How fast did they go in that vehicle?

_____

7. If the speedometer needle on the red racer is pointing to 70, how **fast** is the vehicle going?

_____

8. How **far** will that vehicle go in one hour? _____

C REVIEW ITEMS

1. Write the names of the 8 planets, starting with the planet that's closest to the sun.

_____

_____

_____

2. Each sled in the Iditarod must have room to hold ▊▊▊ .
   - a spare sled
   - another musher
   - food for a week
   - an injured dog

3. According to the Iditarod rules, there must be at least how many dogs on the gangline at the end of the race?
   - 5
   - 9
   - 14
   - 16

4. During the Iditarod, a musher must pack at least _____ extra sets of booties for each dog.

5. During the Iditarod, where must a musher take any dog that is injured?

_____

GO TO PART D IN YOUR TEXTBOOK

A   STORY ITEMS

1. Why doesn't it feel like you're moving when you're speeding through space? _____

2. What is a cloud of stars called? _____

3. What will happen if Al passes the old man's test?

    _____

4. What will happen if Al doesn't pass the test?

    _____

5. Name the 3 vehicles Al and the old man rode in.

    _____

6. How long does it take sound to travel one mile? _____

7. How long did it take the jet plane to travel one mile?

    • less than 5 seconds   • 5 seconds   • more than 5 seconds

8. Why was it so quiet inside the jet plane? _____

    _____

9. How fast did they go in the last vehicle they were in?

    • 9 thousand miles per hour   • 9 thousand miles

    • 4 thousand miles per hour

Look at the names of objects below.

10. Put a **1** next to the thing that travels the slowest.

11. Put a **2** next to the thing that travels the next slowest.

12. Number the rest of the objects to show how fast they travel.

    _____ rocket   _____ racing car   _____ jet plane   _____ light

1. Write **north**, **south**, **east**, and **west** in the correct boxes.

2. In which direction is ocean current F moving? _____

3. In which direction is ocean current G moving? _____

4. Which direction is the wind coming from? _____

5. Make an arrow above ice chunk H to show the direction the current will move the ice chunk.

6. Make an arrow next to ice chunk K to show the direction the current will move the ice chunk.

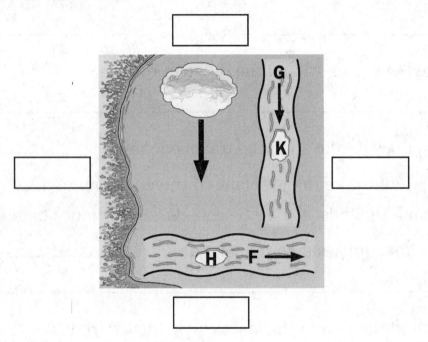

C SKILL ITEMS

Use a prefix to complete each item.

	re		dis
1. arrange	_____		_____
2. appear	_____		_____
3. charge	_____		_____

GO TO PART C IN YOUR TEXTBOOK

A STORY ITEMS

1. Al had trouble going to sleep because ▨▨▨ .
    - he wasn't tired
    - he kept thinking about his trip
    - he was hungry

2. Why did Al leave for school early?
    - to read the newspaper
    - to read his science book
    - to talk to his teacher

3. Why was Al's teacher surprised when he raised his hand in school?

    _____

4. It is so quiet in a jet plane that is going 900 miles per hour because the plane is moving faster than _____ .

5. What was the name of the street the store was on?

    _____

6. What question did the old man ask Al?

    _____

7. Why did the old man say he would take Al on another trip?

    _____

8. What did Al want to learn about on his next trip? _____

9. Al's teacher had told the class that all things are made of _____ .

10. How many states of matter are there? _____

1. Write the missing seasons on the picture below.

2. Shade half of Earth D and half of Earth F.

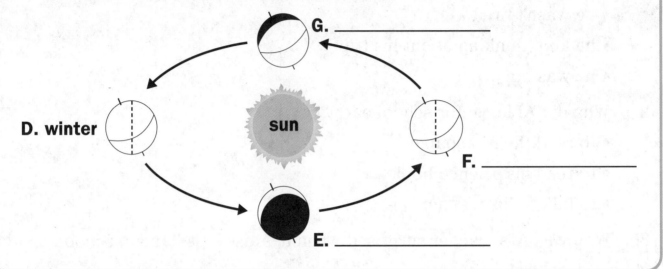

Look at the picture below.

3. Which side of Earth is closer to the sun, **P** or **Q**? _____

4. Which side of Earth is in nighttime? _____

5. Which side of Earth is in daytime? _____

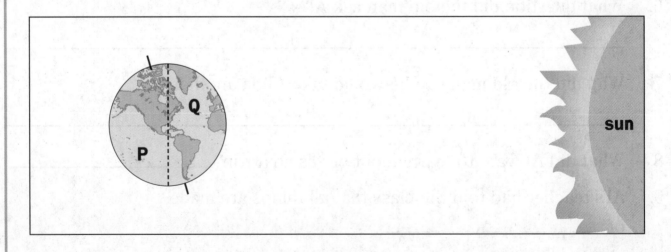

GO TO PART C IN YOUR TEXTBOOK

A STORY ITEMS

1. When things are hard, what state of matter are they?

    _____

2. When hard matter gets hotter, which state does it change into first?

    _____

3. When matter gets still hotter, which state does it change into?

    _____

4. At first, the frying pan was matter in the _____ state.

5. How can you change a solid state of matter into a liquid?

    _____

6. To change a liquid state of matter into a gas, you make the liquid

    _____ .

7. What is the coldest state of matter? _____

8. The sun is matter in the _____ state.

9. What state of matter is a rock? _____

10. What state of matter is the air around you? _____

11. What state of matter did the rock turn into when the old man let go of it?

    _____

12. Look at the list below. Put **M** in front of everything that is matter.

_____ air   _____

_____ water   _____

_____ ice   _____

_____ brick   _____

_____ wood   _____

_____ steam   _____

_____ glass   _____

_____ tea drink   _____

_____ smoke   _____

_____ juice   _____

Look at the list above.

13. Write **solid** after everything that is matter in the solid state.

14. Write **liquid** after everything that is matter in the liquid state.

15. Write **gas** after everything that is matter in the gas state.

B ┃ **SKILL ITEMS**

In the <u>first</u> blank, write the word that means <u>the opposite of</u>.
In the <u>second</u> blank, write the word that means <u>again</u>.

	opposite	again
1. order	_____	_____
2. connect	_____	_____
3. continue	_____	_____

GO TO PART C IN YOUR TEXTBOOK

A STORY ITEMS

1. Al and the old man went to several places with the bottle of air. First they filled the bottle with air on planet _____ .

2. Then Al and the old man took the bottle of air to a place that has rings. What is the name of that place? _____

3. Where did Al and the old man go to next? _____

4. In what state of matter is air on Saturn? _____

5. In what state of matter is air on Earth? _____

6. In what state of matter is air on Pluto? _____

7. Which is colder, Saturn or Pluto? _____

8. Why is it colder there? _____

9. What state of matter is water? _____

10. What state of matter is steam? _____

11. What state of matter is ice? _____

12. How can you change a liquid state of matter into a solid?

_____

13. How can you change a liquid state of matter into a gas?

_____

14. What was strange about Anywhere Street?

_____

15. How did Al feel about himself when he realized that he understood matter? _____

1. **Write the letters** of the 5 things that are matter in the solid state.

   _____

2. **Write the letters** of the 4 things that are matter in the liquid state.

   _____

3. **Write the letters** of the 3 things that are matter in the gas state.

   _____

   a. brick   d. juice   g. smoke   j. wood

   b. glass   e. milk   h. tea drink   k. water

   c. ice   f. rock   i. air   l. steam

4. What state of matter is the air around you? _____

C SKILL ITEMS

Write the word for each description.

1. not clear _____
2. not certain _____
3. not able _____
4. not fair _____

Write the word for each description. Use dis or re.

5. opposite of appear _____
6. start again _____
7. opposite of like _____
8. play again _____

GO TO PART D IN YOUR TEXTBOOK

A STORY ITEMS

1. Why didn't Al tell his mother he had gone to Saturn and Pluto?

   _____

2. Why did Al stay up so late?

   _____

3. What did Al do in school that showed he was very tired?

   _____

4. The old man asked Al two questions. Write one of those questions.

   _____

5. Why did the old man disappear from the store? _____

   _____

6. What is the coldest state of any matter? _____

7. What is the next-coldest state of any matter? _____

8. What is the hottest state of any matter? _____

9. Why didn't Al know the answers to the old man's questions?

   _____

10. What did the sign in the store window usually say?

    _____

11. What did the sign in the store window say after Al failed the test?

    _____

12. Where did Al go to find the answers to the questions the old man asked?

    _____

13. Where did Al go at the end of the chapter?

_____

14. Why did he go there? _____

_____

B REVIEW ITEMS

Draw arrows at **J,** at **K,** and at **L** to show the way the melted rock moves.

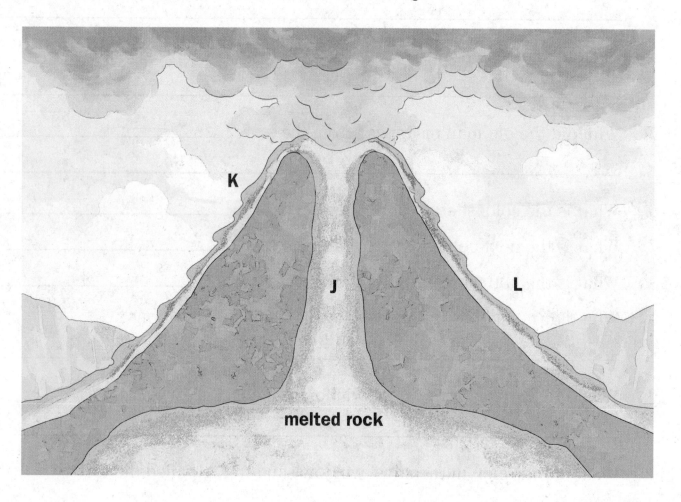

melted rock

GO TO PART C IN YOUR TEXTBOOK

A   STORY ITEMS

1. Why did the old man give Al a harder test?

    _____

2. Did Al pass the harder test? _____

3. Do all things turn into a gas at the same temperature? _____

4. All matter is made up of _____ .

5. After Al passed the test and left the store, what do you think the sign in
    the window said? _____

6. Do sugar molecules look like air molecules? _____

7. Do all sugar molecules look the same? _____

8. What did Al do that surprised his class? _____

    _____

9. What did Al want to see on his next trip? _____

10. Name 5 things that are made up of molecules. _____

    _____

11. Why can't you see molecules when you look at an object? _____

    _____

Earth	binoculars
pressure	light
planets	stars
sun	Jupiter
Pluto	Saturn
moon	gravity
telescope	Io
sunshine	Mars
Neptune	

ACROSS

2. The sun gives heat and ▮▮▮▮▮ to all the planets.

5. The largest planet in the solar system is ▮▮▮▮▮ .

7. This dwarf planet that is cold enough to freeze air is ▮▮▮▮▮ .

8. One of Jupiter's moons is named ▮▮▮▮▮ .

9. The planet we live on is called ▮▮▮▮▮ .

DOWN

1. The force that makes things fall to the ground is ▮▮▮▮▮ .

3. You can look through a ▮▮▮▮▮ to see some planets.

4. The ▮▮▮▮▮ is in the middle of the solar system.

6. There are eight ▮▮▮▮▮ in the solar system.

GO TO PART C IN YOUR TEXTBOOK

A STORY ITEMS

1. How did Al and the old man change to go inside the ice cube?

_____

2. The old man told Al, "An ice cube is made up of space and

_____ ."

3. How were the molecules of the ice cube arranged? _____

4. The molecules that Al saw were in the _____ state of matter.

5. Circle 2 things that tell about any molecules in the solid state.

    • They fly around.   • They are hot.

    • They stay in place.   • They are lined up.

6. The old man planned to make the ice cube colder than the temperature

    on _____ .

B REVIEW ITEMS

Use these names to answer the questions: **Tyrannosaurus, Triceratops.**

1. What is animal G? _____

2. What is animal H? _____

G

H

3. Name an arrow-shaped fish. _____

4. Write **2** facts about those fish. _____

    _____

5. Is the water cooler **at 100 feet down** or **at the surface?**

    _____

6. Is all the water at 100 feet down the same temperature? _____

7. What do you fill a buoyancy device with? _____

8. When the device is filled up, what happens to the diver?

    _____

9. When the device is empty, what happens to the diver?

    _____

C SKILL ITEMS

Write the word for each description.

1. without effort

    _____

2. without a home

    _____

3. paint again

    _____

4. opposite of connect

    _____

5. not zipped

    _____

6. without a hat

    _____

GO TO PART C IN YOUR TEXTBOOK

A STORY ITEMS

1. At the beginning of the story, who got into an argument over the sewing machine? _____

2. Who settled the argument? _____

3. Where are the boys going on their bikes?

   _____

4. Why were they going there?

   _____

5. What did Jamal want to do in the vacant lot?

   _____

6. What had once happened to Sonny when he was riding on a dirt hill?

   _____

7. What happened to Jamal in the vacant lot?

   _____

8. Where did Sonny go for help? _____

9. What did the doctor say that upset Jamal? _____

   _____

10. What did Sonny say he'd do to keep Jamal in shape?

    _____

1. What is the main setting for this story?

   _____

2. Name the 2 main characters in this story.

   _____

3. Write the plot for this story. Tell who Sonny and Jamal are. Tell about their problem. Tell what happened to Jamal and what Sonny did. Tell how Jamal's feelings changed.

   _____

   _____

   _____

   _____

   _____

C SKILL ITEMS

1. A message for this story is "A friend in _____ is a friend indeed."

   When a patient comes to the hospital with an injured leg, the doctor will examine the leg before treating it. If the bone is broken, the doctor might put a cast on the leg or some other device for keeping the bone in one place. Sometimes the treatment will include an operation to set the bones. In order for the treatment to work, it is very important for all weight to be kept off of the broken bone.

2. What is a treatment?
   a. things that help an injured part become healthy again
   b. ice cream and other sweets
   c. a reward for doing a trick

END OF LESSON 110

A   STORY ITEMS

1.   How many globes were in each molecule of the ice cube? _____

2.   How many smaller balls were attached to the center globe? _____

3.   How can you make the molecules in a liquid move faster?

      • Heat them.   • Cool them.

4.   How can you make the molecules in a liquid move slower?

      _____

5.   When ice cube molecules are as cold as they can get, how much do
      they move? _____

6.   Do they move **more** or move **less** at room temperature? _____

7.   In which state of matter do molecules move fastest?

      _____

8.   In which state of matter do molecules move slowest?

      _____

9.   In which state of matter are molecules lined up in rows?

      _____

Triceratops	lava	Tyrannosaurus	whirlpools	storms	China
Mesozoic	Greece	mention	earthquake	blushed	glance
Tokyo	hesitated	suppose	dinosaurs		

ACROSS

3. Hot, melted rock is called ▨▨▨ .

5. A huge killer dinosaur was named ▨▨▨ .

6. Another word for **believe** or **think** is ▨▨▨ .

7. When you look at something very quickly, you ▨▨▨ at the thing.

8. In the Bermuda Triangle, there are many ▨▨▨ .

DOWN

1. Leonard ▨▨▨ when the audience applauded.

2. The animals that lived during the Mesozoic were called ▨▨▨ .

4. The time when dinosaurs lived is called the ▨▨▨ .

5. The largest city in Japan is ▨▨▨ .

GO TO PART C IN YOUR TEXTBOOK

A | STORY ITEMS

1. Al wanted to tell Angela his secret about Anywhere Street, but part of his mind told him that Angela _____

   _____ .

2. Did she believe Al's story about his trips? _____

3. Did Angela believe that Al knew a lot about molecules? _____

4. Why did Al know so much about molecules? _____

   _____

5. Where did Al go after school? _____

6. The old man gave Al a test on molecules. Write the 2 questions the old man asked. Then write the answers to the questions.

   Question 1: _____

   Answer 1: _____

   Question 2: _____

   Answer 2: _____

7. After the test, Al asked the old man a question. What did he want the old man to do? _____

8. How will Angela pay for her trip?

   _____

B | REVIEW ITEMS

1. How many moons does Saturn have? _____

2. How many moons does Jupiter have? _____

3. How far is it from Earth to Jupiter? _____

seconds	twelve	matter	solid	hours
molecules	answer	minutes	respond	cloud
liquid	galaxy	lava	gas	three

ACROSS

2. There are ▢▢▢ states of matter.

3. Tiny parts of matter are called ▢▢▢.

7. Another word for **answer** is ▢▢▢.

9. Hot melted rock is ▢▢▢.

10. It takes light 8 ▢▢▢ to travel from the sun to Earth.

11. When things are hard, they are matter in the ▢▢▢ state.

DOWN

1. Air, water, and dirt are different states of ▢▢▢.

4. Water is matter in the ▢▢▢ state.

5. It takes sound 5 ▢▢▢ to travel one mile.

6. A cloud of stars is called a ▢▢▢.

8. The air around you is matter in the ▢▢▢ state.

GO TO PART C IN YOUR TEXTBOOK

A STORY ITEMS

1. After supper, Al said to Angela, "I want to tell you something, so let's go for a walk." What did he want to tell her?

   _____

2. Al kept creating a picture in his mind of what Angela's face would look like when she found out that Al had been telling the truth. He imagined that her mouth would _____ .

3. He imagined that her eyes would _____ .

4. How did the picture that Al imagined compare to the one that he actually saw?

   _____

5. Was Angela surprised that there really was an Anywhere Street? _____

6. How did Angela feel when the old man first appeared?

   _____

7. Where did the old man take Al and Angela?

   _____

8. Why did Al take off his jacket and open his shirt?

   _____

9. What animal charged at Al and Angela?

   _____

1. What do sled dogs wear to protect their feet? _____

2. Circle the 2 items that tell what could happen to a sled dog's feet if they didn't have protection.

   • snowballs between the pads   • stiff legs

   • long claws   • cuts from ice and frozen snow

3. If booties on a sled dog are too tight, what could happen?

   _____

4. If booties are too loose, what could happen?

   _____

5. What command tells sled dogs to turn right? _____

6. What command tells sled dogs to move straight ahead? _____

7. What command tells sled dogs to turn left? _____

8. During the Iditarod, what does a musher have to do with any dogs that are injured? _____

9. According to the rules, there must be at least how many dogs on the gangline at the end of the Iditarod? _____

C SKILL ITEMS

Write the word for each description.

1. not happy	2. make again	3. opposite of join
_____	_____	_____
4. opposite of honest	5. not ready	6. not well
_____	_____	_____

GO TO PART C IN YOUR TEXTBOOK

A   STORY ITEMS

1. What happened to the elephant that was chasing Angela?

   _____

2. Where did the old man take Al and Angela after they left the jungle?

   _____

3. Who wanted to go there? _____

4. How deep was the **bottom** of the ocean where Al and Angela were?
   - 200 feet
   - 2 miles
   - 20 feet

5. What covers some of the rocks? _____

6. What is coral made of?
   - animal skeletons
   - rocks
   - insects

7. When the old man blew up the balloon, it was about as big as

   _____ .

8. The old man stopped at 30 feet from the surface. As he went up, did the balloon have **more** or **less** air pressure on it? _____

9. So did the balloon get **bigger** or **smaller**? _____

10. Then what happened to the balloon?

    _____

11. Where would a balloon be bigger—at 60 feet below the surface or at 120 feet below the surface?

_____

Here's how big a balloon is at 20 meters below the surface.

X

Here's the same balloon when it is **deeper** or **not as deep.**

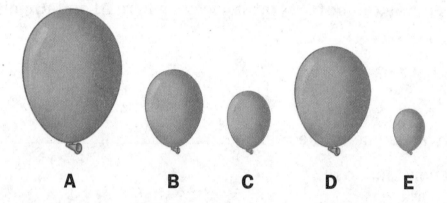

A   B   C   D   E

12. Write **D** on each balloon that is deeper than balloon **X.**

13. **Circle** the balloon that is the **deepest.**

14. **Cross out** the balloon that is **closest to the surface.**

15. What is the old man going to show Al and Angela next?

_____

16. How does Angela feel about that? _____

GO TO PART C IN YOUR TEXTBOOK

A STORY ITEMS

1. Al and Angela saw a huge whale. Name that whale.

   _____

2. The old man told Al and Angela, "The squid moves by

   _____."

3. Name the largest animal in the world. _____

4. That animal weighs more than _____ elephants.

5. Are whales fish? _____

6. Another name for an orca is _____ .

7. Are whales **warm-blooded** or **cold-blooded?**

   _____

---

8. Name the animal in the picture. _____

9. Which arrow shows the way the animal squirts water out? _____

10. Which arrow shows the way the animal will move? _____

11. Make a **T** on a tentacle.

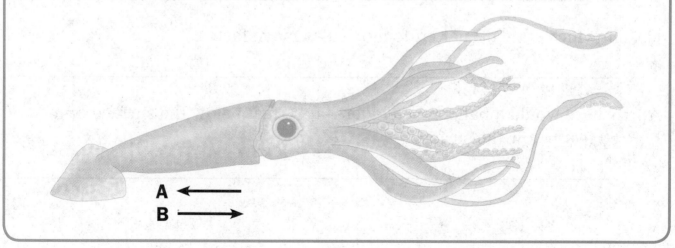

A ←
B →

The picture shows marks left by an animal.

1. Which arrow shows the direction the animal is moving? _____

2. Write the letter of the part that shows the mark left by the animal's tail.

   _____

3. Write the letter of the part that shows a footprint. _____

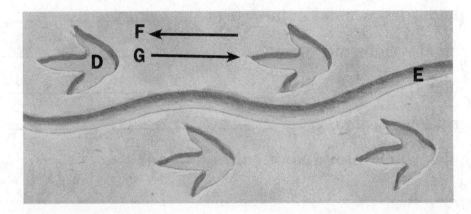

4. In which state of matter are molecules lined up in rows?

   _____

5. In which state of matter do molecules move slowest?

   _____

6. In which state of matter do molecules move fastest?

   _____

7. Where would a balloon be bigger—at 90 feet below the surface or at 60 feet below the surface?

   _____

GO TO PART C IN YOUR TEXTBOOK

A STORY ITEMS

1. One of the killer whales made high beep sounds. What did that tell the other killer whales to do? _____

2. Did the killer whales kill the blue whale? _____

3. How deep is the deepest part of the ocean?
   - 60 miles   • 10 miles   • 6 miles

4. Do plants grow on the bottom of the deepest part of the ocean? _____

5. Tell why. _____

6. Do the fish on the bottom of the ocean look like fish near the surface?

   _____

7. What is animal A? _____

8. What is animal B? _____

9. What is animal C? _____

10. When Al and Angela got home, their mother was holding a package. Who was the package from? _____

11. What was inside the package? _____

12. What was shown in the picture on the cover?

_____

13. Some pictures in the book showed things that Al and Angela had seen on their trip. Name **2** of those things.

_____

_____

14. Where did Al take the book the next day? _____

15. Who made fun of Al in school? _____

16. How did the students in Al's class like his explanations of the things in the book? _____

17. What did the students do when Al finished his talk?

_____

B SKILL ITEMS

Write the word for each description.

1. full of thought

_____

2. opposite of charge

_____

3. without roads

_____

4. think again

_____

5. without care

_____

6. full of care

_____

GO TO PART C IN YOUR TEXTBOOK

A STORY ITEMS

1. Where did Al and Angela go after school?

    _____

2. Why was Angela walking so fast?

    _____

3. The old man asked Al and Angela many questions about the sea. Write 2 of those questions. Then write the answers.

    Question 1: _____

    _____

    Answer 1: _____

    Question 2: _____

    _____

    Answer 2: _____

4. Where did Angela want to go on their next trip?

    _____

5. Name the first star that the old man showed Al and Angela.

    _____

6. Al and Angela saw a flame on the sun that was _____ times bigger than Earth.

7. Al and Angela went to a little star. That star was _____ miles through the middle.

8. Earth is _____ miles through the middle.

9. Which weighs more, the little star or Earth?

   _____

10. The old man put a spoonful of matter on one side of the balance scale. What was the first thing he put on the other side of the scale?

    _____

11. Did the scale balance? _____

12. What object finally made the scale balance?

    _____

13. So the spoonful of matter weighed more than ▢▢▢ .

    • 10 trucks   • a huge mountain   • 50 trucks

B REVIEW ITEMS

1. In what state of matter is air on Pluto? _____

2. In what state of matter is air on Earth? _____

3. In what state of matter is air on Saturn? _____

4. What state of matter is steam? _____

5. What state of matter is water? _____

6. What state of matter is ice? _____

7. How deep is the deepest part of the ocean?

   • 1 mile   • 6 miles   • 10 miles

GO TO PART C IN YOUR TEXTBOOK

A STORY ITEMS

1. Is our sun a **huge** star? _____

2. Al and Angela went to a huge star. Name the planets that would be inside that star if it were in the center of our solar system.

   _____

3. How long would it take light to travel from one side of that star to the other side?

   _____

4. Name the galaxy that Al and Angela saw.

   _____

5. How many stars are in that galaxy?

   _____

6. How long does it take light to travel from one side of that galaxy to the other side?

   • 100 thousand years   • 180 thousand years   • 40 years

7. One star in the galaxy started flashing. What's special about that star?

   _____

B SKILL ITEMS

Write the word for each description.

1. being hard _____
2. full of thought _____
3. without thought _____
4. being bright _____
5. not happy _____
6. without a point _____

C CROSSWORD PUZZLE

temperature	pressure	giant	blue	squid	killer
thousand	hundred	skeletons	shells	coral	plants
exclaimed	twenty	selected	two	tentacles	selects

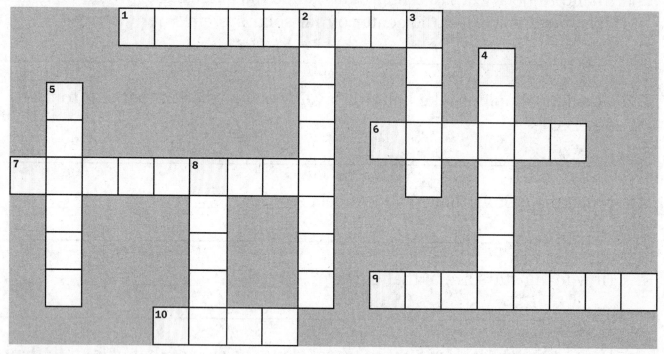

ACROSS

1. Coral is made up of ▓▓▓ of sea animals.

6. ▓▓▓ **whales** are also called orcas.

7. The arms of a squid are called ▓▓▓ .

9. The old man used a balloon to show Al and Angela how ▓▓▓ works.

10. The largest animal in the world is the ▓▓▓ whale.

DOWN

2. Earth is 8 ▓▓▓ miles through the middle.

3. A sea animal that looks like a giant tube with many arms is a ▓▓▓ .

4. Another word for **chooses** is ▓▓▓ .

5. A blue whale weighs as much as ▓▓▓ elephants.

8. Some rocks under water are covered with ▓▓▓ .

GO TO PART C IN YOUR TEXTBOOK

A STORY ITEMS

1. The teacher told the class that on Monday they would have a test on

    _____ .

2. Was Al excited about the test? _____

3. Did Al want to learn about the human body? _____

4. As the man's arm pushed the weight overhead, the muscle on the back of
    the arm got [____] .

    • shorter and thicker

    • longer and thicker

    • longer and thinner

5. Why were the store windows decorated?

    _____

6. Why did Al feel sad when he looked inside those windows?

    _____

    _____

7. What present did Al want to buy for his mother?

    _____

8. Who decided where to go on the next trip? _____

9. At the end of the chapter, what did the old man do to one of the muscles?

    _____

10. Name the muscle on the **front** of the upper arm. _____

11. Name the muscle on the **back** of the upper arm. _____

12. How many jobs does each muscle have? _____

13. Name the arm muscle that gets shorter when you straighten your arm.

_____

14. Name the arm muscle that gets shorter when you bend your arm.

_____

15. When you bend your arm, one of the muscles gets longer as the other one gets shorter. Name the muscle that gets longer. _____

16. Which letter shows the triceps? _____
17. Which letter shows the biceps? _____
18. Which letter shows the muscle that bends the arm? _____
19. Which letter shows the muscle that straightens the arm? _____

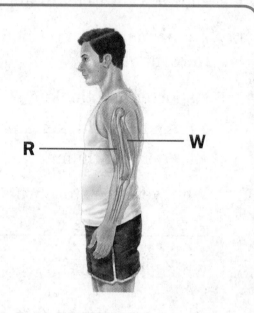

R ——————————— W

GO TO PART C IN YOUR TEXTBOOK

A SETTING, CHARACTERS, PLOT

1. What is the main setting for this story? _____

2. Name the two main characters in this story.

    _____

3. Write the plot for this story. Tell about the soldier's problem. Tell how he meets the family. Tell what the soldier did with the soup stone. Tell how the soup was made.

    _____

    _____

    _____

    _____

    _____

B STORY ITEMS

1. Who had the idea for making soup? _____

2. What was the first thing that went into the water? _____

3. What went into the pot next? _____

4. Name 4 other things they added to the water.

    _____

5. Where did the onions come from? _____

6. Who brought the rabbits? _____

7. How many people ate the soup? _____

8. Was there enough soup for everyone? _____

9. What did the soldier give the woman at the end of the story?

_____

10. Where did the soldier get another one? _____

Answer these questions about *The Soup Stone*.

1. What is the lesson of the fable about the soup stone?

_____

2. In the story *The Soup Stone,* how did the soldier start the soup?

_____

3. How did the water turn into soup?

_____

4. What was the soup like when it was done?

_____

Write ways that the story *The Soup Stone* could be different if it took place today.

1. The people cooked over a fire.

_____

2. The woman's son hunted for meat.

_____

3. The people kept carrots under a bench.

_____

END OF LESSON 120

A STORY ITEMS

1. Most muscles are attached to _____ .

2. What happened when the old man removed the bones from the model's legs? _____

3. What is the skeleton of the human body made of?

   • bones   • skin   • muscles

4. How many bones are in the adult human body? _____

5. Circle the 2 things that bones do.

   • protect body parts

   • make the body move

   • get shorter and thicker

   • make the body strong

6. Did Angela like how the skeleton looked? _____

7. How many bones make up the skull? _____

8. What do those bones protect? _____

9. What would happen if something hit the **back** of your brain?

   _____

10. What would happen if something hit the **lower part** of your brain?

   _____

11. What body parts do the ribs protect? _____ and

   _____

12. Your heart is about as big as your _____ .

13. What might happen if something hurt your lungs?

_____

14. Does Al want to learn more about the body? _____

15. Had Al wanted to learn about the body before this trip started? _____

16. At the end of the chapter, Al and Angela were inside a large tube that

was filled with _____ .

B REVIEW ITEMS

1. Name the largest planet in the solar system. _____

2. How long does it take Jupiter to spin around one time?

_____

3. How long does it take light to travel from the sun to Earth?

_____

4. Where would a balloon be bigger—at 40 feet below the surface of the
ocean or at 80 feet below the surface?

_____ .

5. Are whales fish? _____

6. Are whales **warm-blooded** or **cold-blooded?**

_____

GO TO PART D IN YOUR TEXTBOOK

A GLOSSARY AND GUIDE WORDS

1.
caretaker	gardener

2.
friends	holiday

Write the letters that words on these pages could begin with.

3.
buns	fix

_____

4.
telephone	word

_____

B STORY ITEMS

1. At the beginning of the chapter, Al and Angela were floating in a tube. What is that tube called? _____

2. Name the liquid that was in the tube. _____

3. What color was that liquid? _____

4. What was making the great pounding sound that Al and Angela heard?

_____

5. Why was the pounding sound getting louder? _____

_____

6. What happens to the blood when the heart pounds?

_____

7. The old man told Al and Angela what the heart does. He told them that the heart _____ through the body.

8. What are the doors in the heart made of? _____

9. Which chamber of the heart was bigger, the first one or the second one?

   _____

10. How many doors were in the second chamber? _____

11. You can hear two sounds in the heart. The blood makes the little sound when it leaves the little _____ .

12. When does it make the big sound?

   _____

13. When Al and Angela left the heart, they were in another blood vessel. What was different about how the blood moved in that blood vessel?

    • Things kept starting and stopping.

    • Things moved at the same speed.

    • Things moved very slowly.

14. Where was that blood vessel going?

    • from the body   • to the heart   • to the lungs

15. What does blood get in the lungs?

    • water   • oxygen   • food

16. Things can't burn without _____ .

17. In the lungs, the blood changed from _____ red to _____ red.

18. What color is blood that does not have oxygen? _____

19. What color is blood that has fresh oxygen? _____

GO TO PART C IN YOUR TEXTBOOK

A STORY ITEMS

1. When Angela and Al left the lungs, they were in a blood vessel. Where was the blood vessel going?

   _____

2. What color was the blood around them when they left the lungs?

   _____

3. Why was the blood that color?

   _____

4. How many chambers does the heart have? _____

5. How many chambers did Al and Angela go through **before** they went to the lungs? _____

6. How many chambers did they go through **after** they went to the lungs?

   _____

7. Where does dark red blood go after it leaves the heart?

   _____

8. Then the blood goes back to the _____ .

9. Then the blood goes to the _____ .

10. Why does oxygen blood have to go back to the heart after it leaves the lungs? _____

    _____

11. Muscles are made up of tiny _____ .

12. When the oxygen left the blood, the blood changed from
_____ to _____ .

13. Muscle cells need _____ to work.

Draw lines to match the words below.

14. These blood vessels
pound every time the •
heart beats.

            • blood vessels that lead from
the heart

15. These blood vessels
do not pound. •

            • blood vessels that lead to
the heart

16. These blood vessels
look blue under •
your skin.

---

17. Blood vessels that look blue under the skin are actually filled with
_____ red blood.

---

18. Did Angela want to take the trip around the body again? _____

19. Tell why. _____

_____

Copyright © McGraw-Hill Education

GO TO PART C IN YOUR TEXTBOOK

A STORY ITEMS

1. What do nerves do?

    • carry messages

    • carry blood

    • carry oxygen

2. In which part of the man's body did Angela and Al start following the nerve?

    • big toe   • knee   • hand

3. What did the pulses in the nerve feel like to Al?

    • big electric shocks

    • tiny electrical pulses

    • heavy pounding

4. Were there **more pulses** or **fewer pulses** when the man started tying his shoe? _____

5. When the nerve part going to the brain was cut, how many pulses did the brain receive?

    _____

6. When would the nerves in your hand pulse faster—**when you're asleep** or **when you burn your hand?**

    _____

7. When the old man cut the nerve part going from the brain to the thumb, the man ▆▆▆ .

    • could not move his thumb   • could not feel his thumb

8. When the old man cut the nerve part going from the thumb to the brain, the man ▆▆▆ .

    • could not move his thumb   • could not feel his thumb

B CROSSWORD PUZZLE

numb	triceps
biceps	ice
ribs	skull
air	heart
lungs	oxygen
imagination	nerves
cerebrum	bones
steam	paralyzed

ACROSS

1. The muscle that bends the arm is the ▩ .

4. If you can't move a part of your body, that part is ▩ .

5. Your ▩ protect your lungs and your heart.

8. Your ▩ pumps blood through your body.

9. If something hurt your ▩ , you wouldn't be able to breathe.

10. Most muscles are attached to ▩ .

DOWN

2. The part of your mind that can think of things that might happen is your ▩ .

3. The gas state of water is ▩ .

6. Your ▩ protects your brain.

7. Things can't burn without ▩ .

GO TO PART C IN YOUR TEXTBOOK

A INFORMATION ITEMS

1. What happens to light when it goes through a magnifying glass?

   • It goes straight.   • It goes faster.   • It bends.

2. If you make a picture of a tree using a magnifying glass, the top of the tree will be at the _____ of the picture.

3. The eye is like a _____ .

4. Where does light enter the eyeball?

   • front   • side   • back

5. Where does the picture form?

   • front   • side   • back

B STORY ITEMS

1. What do nerves that lead from the brain to the hand tell the hand?

   _____

2. What do nerves that lead from the hand to the brain tell the brain?

   _____

3. What is your backbone made of?

   • one long bone   • little hollow bones   • rib bones

4. Name the bundle of nerves that goes up and down through the middle of your backbone. _____

5. What's strange about the bones in the backbone?

   • They are hollow.   • They are solid.   • They are soft.

6. When Al and Angela left the spinal cord, they entered the

    _____ .

7. What does your cerebrum do? _____

8. When Al and Angela first entered the brain, they were in a part that controls some things the body does without thinking. Name 2 of those things.

    _____

9. When Al and Angela moved up through the brain, they came to another part. Did that part have **more nerves** or **fewer nerves?**

    _____

10. Name that part of the brain. _____

11. Which part of your brain works when you think about what you are seeing? _____

C SKILL ITEMS

Write the word for each description.

1. one who plays _____
2. one who washes _____
3. not washed _____
4. being light _____

5. opposite of agree _____
6. without a clue _____
7. one who speaks _____

GO TO PART D IN YOUR TEXTBOOK

A   INFORMATION ITEMS

Draw lines to show where the paths of light will go when they go through the cornea and lens.

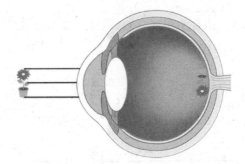

B   STORY ITEMS

1. What did the old man do to scare the man?

   _____

2. What happened to the nerves in the man's brain?

   • They pulsed more rapidly.

   • They pulsed more slowly.

   • They became cooler.

3. What did the nerves do after the lion disappeared?

   • They pulsed more rapidly.

   • They pulsed more slowly.

   • They became cooler.

4. The nerves from the eye go to the ▮▮▮▮ of the brain.

   • front   • side   • back

5. After Al and Angela left the brain, they went inside a great round chamber. What was that chamber?

    • the heart   • the eye   • the lungs

6. What is the name of the round window in the chamber that can let in a little light to a lot of light? _____

7. On which part of the man's eye could Al and Angela see an image of what the man was looking at?

    • pupil   • retina   • lens   • cornea

8. What was strange about the image they saw?

    _____

9. While Al and Angela were looking at the image, the man's shoes got bigger. Tell why.

    _____

C REVIEW ITEMS

1. Name the bundle of nerves that goes up and down through the middle of your backbone. _____

2. What's strange about the bones in the backbone?

    • They are square.
    • They are hollow.
    • They are soft.

3. When you think, what part of your brain are you using?

    _____

GO TO PART D IN YOUR TEXTBOOK

A STORY ITEMS

1. The retina is covered with ▮▮▮▮ .

    • nerves   • hair   • muscles

2. Each nerve in the retina feels the light and sends a message to the

    _____ .

3. What would a person see if the big nerves from the eyes to the brain

    were cut? _____

4. What do the cornea and lens of your eye do to light?

    • bend it   • change the colors   • make it brighter

5. What is the chamber inside the ear shaped like?

    • a box   • a spiral   • a circle

6. What is the inside of the ear's chamber lined with?

    _____

7. What is each hair inside the ear connected to?

    _____

8. When the hair moves, the nerve _____ .

9. What happens if the hair vibrates very hard?

    • The nerve vibrates hard.

    • The nerve vibrates a little bit.

    • The nerve feels colors.

10. What kinds of sounds are picked up in the biggest part of the chamber—

    high sounds or low sounds? _____

11. What kinds of sounds are picked up in the smallest part of the chamber—

    high sounds or low sounds? _____

Write **big** or **small** to tell which part of your ear chamber would pick up each sound.

12. Big church bell _____

13. Low voice _____

14. Very high voice _____

15. High whistle _____

B   REVIEW ITEMS

1. What does light entering the eyeball pass through after the cornea and before the lens? _____

2. Where does the picture form? _____

3. The nerves from the eye go to the ▨ of the brain.
    • top   • back   • front

4. On which part of the man's eye could Al and Angela see an image of what the man was looking at?
    • lens   • retina   • pupil   • cornea

5. The more water the glass has, the ▨ the sound it makes.
    • lower   • higher

6. **Underline** the glass that will make the lowest ring.

7. **Circle** the glass that will make the highest ring.

A   B   C   D   E   F

GO TO PART C IN YOUR TEXTBOOK

A STORY ITEMS

1. After the trip, the old man gave Al and Angela a book. What was the title of the book?

   _____

2. Why did he give the book to them?

   _____

3. Did the old man want the book back? _____

4. When will the old man give Al and Angela their test on the human body?

   _____

5. Was there snow on the ground when Al and Angela left the old man's store?

   _____

6. About how much snow was on the ground the next morning?

   _____

7. What did Al's mother ask him to do the next morning?

   _____

8. Who worked with Al? _____

CROSSWORD PUZZLE

spiral	numb	nerve	curved	blind
backbone	pupil	vessel	retina	hairs
paralyzed	four	cerebrum	bright	dark

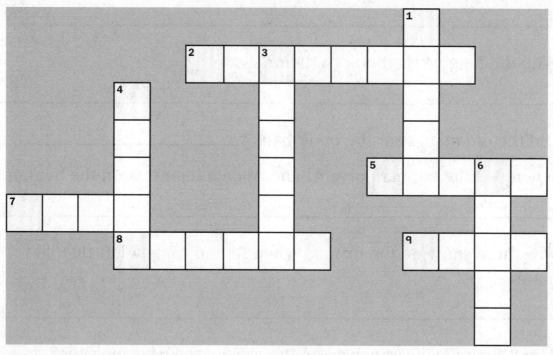

ACROSS

2. The part of the brain that does the thinking is the ▓▓▓▓ .

5. A person who cannot see is ▓▓▓▓ .

7. The heart has ▓▓▓▓ chambers.

8. The chamber inside the ear is shaped like a ▓▓▓▓ .

9. Blood that does not have fresh oxygen is ▓▓▓▓ red.

DOWN

1. The hole at the front of the eye is called the ▓▓▓▓ .

3. The part of the eye where pictures are formed is called the ▓▓▓▓ .

4. The ear's chamber is lined with ▓▓▓▓ .

6. Something in your body that carries messages is a ▓▓▓▓ .

GO TO PART C IN YOUR TEXTBOOK

A INFORMATION ITEMS

1. Look at the picture below. Is the side of the Earth that's closest to the sun **in daylight** or **in darkness?** _____

2. Is the North Pole tilting **toward the sun** or **away from the sun?**

   _____

3. So does this picture show our **summer** or our **winter?** _____

4. As the Earth turns around, which person is in darkness all the time? _____

5. Which person is in daylight all the time? _____

6. Write the letters of all the persons who are in daylight some of the time and darkness some of the time. _____

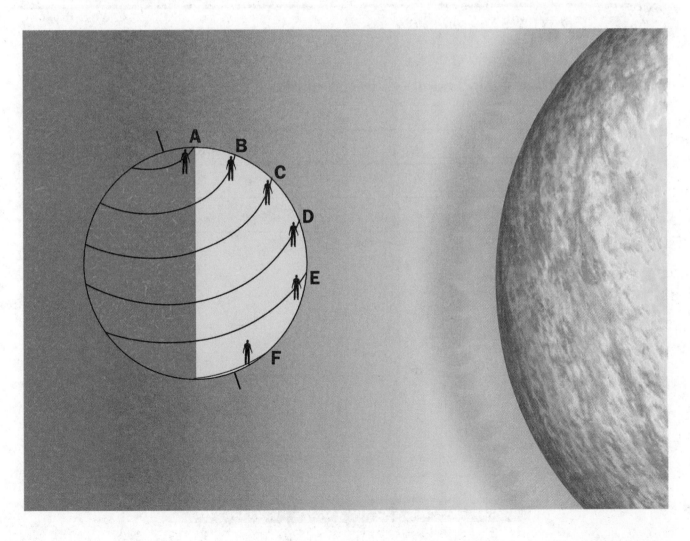

B STORY ITEMS

1. Who made fun of Al in school? _____

2. How many questions were on the test that Al took in school? _____

3. What were most of the questions about? _____

4. Who did better on the test, Homer or Al? _____

5. What grade did Al get on the test? _____

6. How many questions did Angela miss? _____

7. Why didn't the old man give a test to Al and Angela?

_____

_____

C REVIEW ITEMS

Write the missing numbers in the blanks.

_____0_____ feet		surface pressure
1. _____ feet		2 times surface pressure
2. _____ feet		3 times surface pressure
3. _____ feet		4 times surface pressure

GO TO PART D IN YOUR TEXTBOOK

A   STORY ITEMS

1. What was the narrator's trip name in this story? _____

2. Where did she live? _____

3. Where did she and her parents go on vacation?

   _____

4. Who were the guides? _____

5. What were Foo Foo's goals at the beginning of the trip?

   _____

   _____

6. Did Foo Foo meet those goals? _____

7. What goal did she add at the end of the trip?

   _____

8. What did the rafters do with their garbage?

   _____

9. Name 3 animals that Foo Foo saw on the trip.

   _____

10. Name 3 other interesting things Foo Foo saw on the trip. _____

    _____

    _____

11. What did Foo Foo lose during the trip? _____

12. What did the rafters see in the cavern? _____

13. What did Foo Foo do for good luck before going through
    Lava Falls? _____

14. Name 3 things the rafters find in the water. _____

_____

1. What is the main setting for this story? _____

2. Name the main character in this story. _____

3. Write the plot for this story. Tell about the family's vacation plans. Tell why Foo Foo didn't want to go. Tell about the vacation. Tell how Foo Foo's feelings changed.

_____

_____

_____

_____

_____

_____

C STORY THEMES

Match each title below with the theme that fits the story.

1.   *Steps* •   • People often fear the unknown.

2. *My (Wow!) Summer Vacation* •   • Don't judge people too quickly.

3.   *Boar Out There* •   • People aren't always who they appear to be.

4. *The Emperor's New Clothes* •   • New experiences can be fun.

END OF LESSON 130

A STORY ITEMS

1. Who decided where to go on the next trip?

   _____

2. Where did they go? _____

3. Why was it dark there?

   • It was winter.   • It was summer.

4. Why did Al's eyes start to burn?

   _____

5. What was the temperature at the North Pole?

   _____

6. What would that cold air do if you breathed too hard?

   _____

   _____

7. How much daylight is there during winter at the North Pole?

   _____

8. How much nighttime is there during summer at the North Pole?

   _____

9. What season do we have when the North Pole tilts **toward** the sun?

   _____

10. What season do we have when the North Pole tilts **away from** the sun?

    _____

The old man made three tiny forms appear at the North Pole of the model Earth. Fill in the blanks with **dark** or **light.**

11. When it was **summer,** those forms stayed on the

_____ half of Earth.

12. When it was **winter,** those forms stayed on the

_____ half of Earth.

B REVIEW ITEMS

1. Muscles are made up of tiny _____ .

2. Blood vessels that look blue are actually filled with ▬▬▬ .

   • dark red blood   • bright red blood   • dark blue blood

3. Muscle cells need _____ to work.

Use these words to answer the questions:
   • blood vessels that lead from the heart
   • blood vessels that lead to the heart

4. Which blood vessels are dark red? _____

_____

5. Which blood vessels pound every time the heart beats? _____

_____

6. Which blood vessels do not pound? _____

_____

GO TO PART C IN YOUR TEXTBOOK

A STORY ITEMS

1. Do any two snowflakes look **exactly** alike? _____

2. All snowflakes have _____ spokes.

3. The old man made each snowflake as big as a

   _____ .

4. About how deep is the icy snow on a high ridge at the North Pole?

   _____

5. What is under the icy snow at the North Pole?

   _____

6. Which would be harder, snow that is **30 feet below** the top of a pile or snow that is **45 feet below** the top of the pile?

   _____

7. How much land is under the North Pole? _____

8. How many states in the United States are as big as the North Pole?

   _____

1. The picture shows the sun and two globes. Fix up the globes so that half of each globe is in sunlight and half is in shadow.

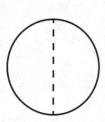  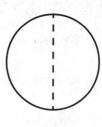

sun

2. **Write the letter** of the thing that travels the slowest. _____

3. **Write the letter** of the thing that travels the fastest. _____

    a. light   c. jet plane   e. rocket

    b. racing car   d. sound

4. Write the letters of the 5 things that are matter in the solid state.

    _____

5. Write the letters of the 4 things that are matter in the liquid state.

    _____

6. Write the letters of the 3 things that are matter in the gas state.

    _____

    a. rock   d. air   g. brick   j. wood

    b. smoke   e. water   h. tea drink   k. juice

    c. glass   f. milk   i. ice   l. steam

GO TO PART C IN YOUR TEXTBOOK

A   INFORMATION ITEMS

1. Draw lines to show where the paths of light will go after they go through the lens.

2. Make an **F** in the box that shows where the film is in a film camera.

3. Make an **L** in the box that shows where the lens is.

4. Make an **I** in the box that shows where the iris is.

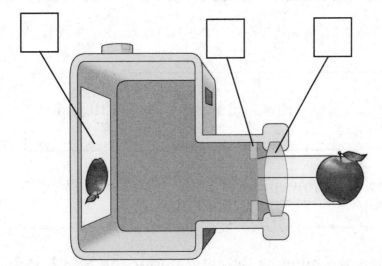

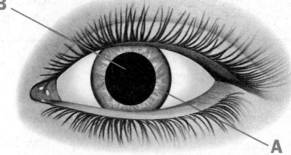

5. What is part A? _____

6. What is part B? _____

1. Fill in the blanks with **toward** or **away from**.

   During our winter, the North Pole tilts _____

   the sun, and the South Pole tilts _____
   the sun.

2. Fill in the blanks with **dark** or **light**.

   During our winter, the North Pole is always _____

   and the South Pole is always _____ .

3. How many hours does it take the sun to make a full circle at the poles?

   _____

4. What's under all the snow and ice at the North Pole?

   _____

5. What's under the snow and ice at the South Pole?

   _____

6. How many square miles is the land under the South Pole?

   • 1 million   • 5 hundred   • 5 million

7. About how deep is the snow and ice at the South Pole?

   _____

8. Where is the snow and ice deeper, at the North Pole or at the South Pole?

   _____

GO TO PART D IN YOUR TEXTBOOK

A STORY ITEMS

1. A man gave Al and Angela each 10 dollars. Tell why.

   _____

   _____

2. Why was the man in a hurry to get his car moving?

   _____

3. Why did Al want to get some more money?

   _____

4. About how deep was the snow in front of Al and Angela's house?

   _____

5. Why were the schools going to be closed the next day?

   _____

6. How had Al felt about school before the old man's trips?

   _____

7. How does Al feel about school now?

   _____

8. Why does he feel that way about school now?

   • He's a poor student.   • He's a good student.

   • He doesn't like school.

9. What is Angela and Al's last name? _____

10. What was the title of the book Al and Angela got in this chapter?

    _____

11. Who sent the book to them? _____

12. The ship named Endurance was stuck in ice at the

    _____ .

13. How many men on that ship died? _____

14. What happened to Robert Scott and the men with him?

    _____

15. What was strange about the food in Robert Scott's camp when people found it fifty years later?

    _____

B   REVIEW ITEMS

1. What is each hair inside the ear connected to? _____

2. What kinds of sounds are picked up in the biggest part of the ear chamber—high sounds or low sounds?

   _____

3. What part of a camera bends the light that goes through it?

   _____

4. What part of a camera lets just enough light into the camera?

   _____

GO TO PART C IN YOUR TEXTBOOK

A INFORMATION ITEMS

1. What are groups of baboons called? _____

2. Name an animal that looks something like a baboon but is the largest
    animal in the ape family.

    _____

3. Name an animal in the cat family that is the size of a big dog.

    _____

4. Name an animal that some people think is the smartest animal in the ocean.

    _____

5. Circle the ocean animals that are warm-blooded.

    • dolphin   • squid   • barracuda

            • blue whale   • orca

6. How long ago did saber-toothed tigers disappear from Earth?

    _____

7. It is called a **saber-toothed tiger** because it had _____
    like sabers.

B STORY ITEMS

1. What did Al want to read about at the library?

    _____

2. Was the library open? _____

3. Why were most of the stores closed? _____

_____

4. Where did Al and Angela go after breakfast?

_____

5. What did the old man want Al and Angela to do when they first got to

his store? _____

6. What did the old man give each of them for doing that?

_____

7. Did Al and Angela go to the store next door at the same time?

_____

8. What was the store next door filled with when Al went there?

_____

9. What was the store filled with when Angela went there?

_____

10. What did Al buy for his mother? _____

11. What did Al buy for Angela? _____

12. How much did **each present** cost? _____

13. What did Angela buy for Al? _____

14. What did Angela buy for her mother? _____

GO TO PART D IN YOUR TEXTBOOK

A STORY ITEMS

1. Why did Al need the old man's trips when he first came to the store?

   _____

   _____

2. Why doesn't Al need the trips anymore? _____

   _____

3. Who decided where to go on this trip?

   _____

4. Where did they go? _____

5. About how many books were in the library?

   • 30 million   • 2 million   • 3 million

6. About how many of those books were about animals?

   • 3 thousand   • 3 hundred   • 3 million

7. What did Angela want to read about? _____

8. Did the old man order **one book** or **more than one?**

   _____

9. What was the title of the first book the old man chose?

   _____

10. Who will start reading from that book? _____

1. What is animal A? _____

2. What is animal B? _____

3. What is animal C? _____

4. What is animal D? _____

5. What is animal E? _____

GO TO PART C IN YOUR TEXTBOOK

A ▎ STORY ITEMS

1. What are the 2 kinds of seasons that Africa has?

   _____

2. What is the savanna of Africa? _____

3. Name 3 kinds of animals that live on the savanna in Africa.

   _____

4. Every day during the dry season, African animals go to a place where they drink. Name that place. _____

5. Did Al and Angela get to read the whole book about animals at water holes? _____

6. What did the old man say they should do if they wanted to read more of the book? _____

7. Why do troops of baboons need lookouts?

   _____

   _____

8. Al said, I never thought of a rock as a _____ before.

9. Al and the old man read part of a book titled *How Animals Learn*. Which animal did the author of that book think is next-smartest after humans?

   _____

10. What animal do you think is the smartest animal? Why?

    _____

11. What animal do you think is the next-smartest animal? Why?

    _____

B CROSSWORD PUZZLE

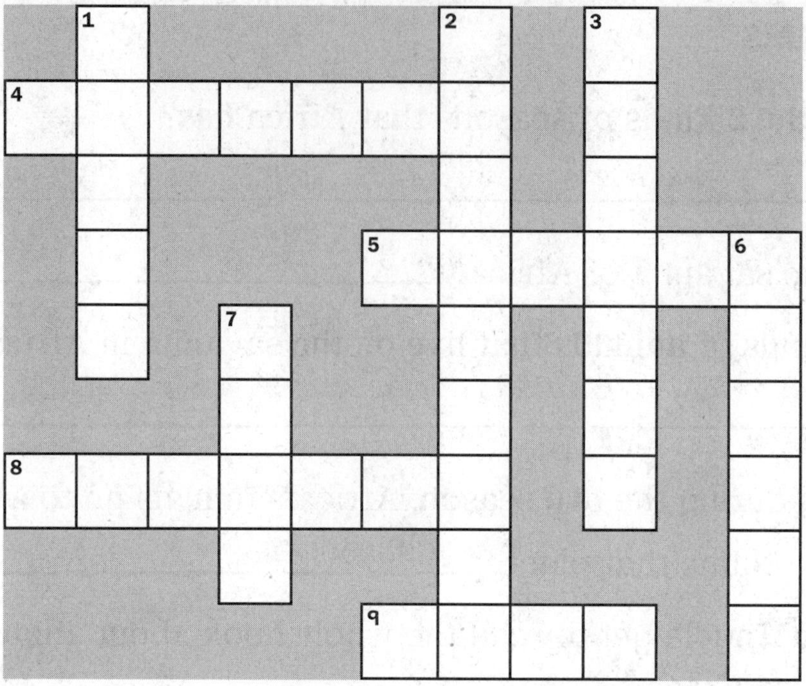

retina	dolphin	iris	sunset	orca	pupil
lens	summer	shark	horizon	film	
extend	Endurance	examine	south	north	

ACROSS

4. Name a warm-blooded ocean animal that is very, very smart.
5. When the North Pole tilts toward the sun, we are having _____ .
8. The place where the sky meets the ground is called the _____ .
9. The part of a camera that bends the light is the _____ .

DOWN

1. The pole at the bottom of the earth is called the _____ Pole.
2. A ship that sank at the South Pole was named the _____ .
3. When you look at something very closely, you _____ that thing.
6. The part of an eye where pictures are formed is the _____ .
7. The part of a camera that lets just enough light in is the _____ .

GO TO PART C IN YOUR TEXTBOOK

A STORY ITEMS

1. Which dinosaur lived **earlier,** Eoraptor or Tyrannosaurus?

   _____

2. About how long was Eoraptor?

   _____

3. Why did Angela want to read about the solar system?

   _____

4. Did Al and Angela like the trip to the library as much as the other trips?

   _____

5. How many books about dinosaurs did the library have?

   • over 600   • over 1000   • fewer than 50

6. Dinosaurs lived during the _____ .

7. Match the items below.

   The Mesozoic began   •   • 2.5 million years ago.

   Dinosaurs appeared   •   • 230 million years ago.

   Saber-toothed tigers appeared •   • 250 million years ago.

8. Write 3 things that you would see in the jungle where the first dinosaurs lived.

   _____

   _____

9. The old man told Al and Angela, "You have to use your

   _____ to take a trip from a book."

10. Name 2 things that were different when Al and Angela left the old man's store.

_____

_____

11. What did Al do after dinner?

_____

12. What was special about the next day?

_____

1. Which iris is right for taking a picture in a dark place? _____

X   Y

2. Which iris sees well in a dark place? _____

C   D

GO TO PART C IN YOUR TEXTBOOK

A STORY ITEMS

1. What did Al's mother give Al for Christmas?

   _____

2. What did Al's family do after breakfast?

   _____

3. Did Al's mother think there was an Anywhere Street? _____

4. Was Al's mother right? _____

5. What was the **real** name of the street?

   _____

6. What kind of store did the old man have?

   _____

7. What kind of book did the old man give Al's mother?

   _____

8. What was the title of the book the old man gave Al and Angela?

   _____

B REVIEW ITEMS

1. The dinosaurs lived in the _____ .

2. Which dinosaur lived earlier, Eoraptor or Tyrannosaurus?

   _____

3. About how long was Eoraptor?

_____

4. Write 3 things that you would see in the jungle where the first dinosaurs lived.

_____

_____

5. What is animal A? _____

6. What is animal B? _____

7. What is animal C? _____

8. What is animal D? _____

9. What is animal E? _____

A

B

C

D

E

GO TO PART D IN YOUR TEXTBOOK

A FAVORITE 3 SELECTIONS

- Choose your top 3 selections. Rank your number-one choice as **1**, your second choice as **2**, and your third choice as **3**.

- If your selection is a story, write **story**. If your selection is a poem, write **poem**. If your selection is the play, that word is already filled in.

Lesson	Title	Author	Rank	Type
10	*The Velveteen Rabbit*	José Reyes		story
20	*Dreams*	Langston Hughes		
20	*The Runner*	Faustin Charles		
30	*The Emperor's New Clothes*	Lucas Novak		
40	*Why Leopard Has Black Spots*	Told by Won-Ldy Paye		
50	*Boar Out There*	Cynthia Rylant		
60	*Spaghetti*	Cynthia Rylant		
70	*Mr. Benton's Dream*	José Reyes		
80	*The Pancake Collector*	Jack Prelutsky		
90	*A Good Day?*	Sooz Gladfelter		
100	*A Lucky Thing*	Alice Schertle		poem
100	*The New Kid*	Mike Makley		
110	*Steps*	Deborah M. Newton Chocolate		
120	*The Soup Stone*	Retold by Maria Leach		
130	*My (Wow!) Summer Vacation*	Susan Cornell Poskanzer		
140	*The Story of Daedalus and Icarus*	Fran Lehr		play

My number-one selection is _____ .

It was written by _____ .

1. **Plot**

   _____

   _____

   _____

   _____

2. **Style**

   _____

   _____

   _____

   _____

3. **Theme**

   _____

   _____

   _____

   _____

END OF LESSON 140

Fact Game Scorecard Sheet

Fact Game for Test 11

1	2	3	4	5
6	7	8	9	10
11	12	13	14	15
16	17	18	19	20

Fact Game for Test 12

1	2	3	4	5
6	7	8	9	10
11	12	13	14	15
16	17	18	19	20

Fact Game for Test 13

1	2	3	4	5
6	7	8	9	10
11	12	13	14	15
16	17	18	19	20

Fact Game for Test 14

1	2	3	4	5
6	7	8	9	10
11	12	13	14	15
16	17	18	19	20

Thermometer Chart

for Check 20 through Check 27

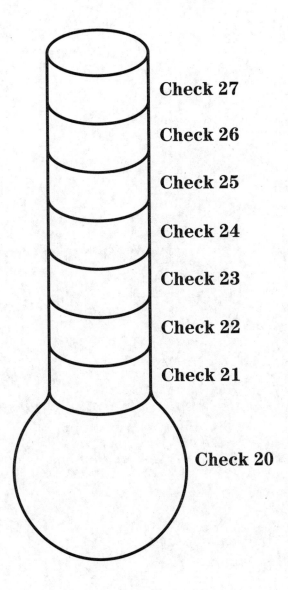

Check 27

Check 26

Check 25

Check 24

Check 23

Check 22

Check 21

Check 20